God Made Something Out of Nothing to Do . . .

and So Can You!

by
Timothy La Belle

Paulist Press
New York/Mahwah, N.J.

Author dedication

In loving memory of Betty La Belle and Red Mooney.
Both were surely God's hands in my life.
I love them both.
And with thanks to my mother, my father, my sisters, and my wife.

Caseside illustrations by Timothy La Belle
Caseside and book design by Saija Autrand, Faces Type & Design

Library of Congress Cataloging-in-Publication Data

LaBelle, Timothy.
God made something out of nothing to do . . . and so can you! / Timothy LaBelle.
p. cm.
ISBN 0-8091-6683-6
1. Creation—Juvenile literature. [1. Creation. 2. Creative ability.] I. Title.

BT695.L33 2000
231.7'65—dc21

00-049158

Published by Paulist Press
997 Macarthur Boulevard
Mahwah, New Jersey 07430

www.paulistpress.com

Printed and bound in Mexico

Once upon a time,
quite a long time ago,
there was nothing to walk on,
there was nowhere to go.

There were no stars
in the heavens,
no birds in the trees,

No grass on the ground,
there were no fish
in the seas.

There weren't any colors.
No skies to call blue.
There was no one there.
There was nothing to do.

So God, who is great, said:
“Hey, have I got a plan!
I’ll make a world full of creatures
and make one of them man!”

Yes, God made a world and
he packed it with life.
Next he made Adam,
and Eve as his wife.

God looked at his work,
and boy was he glad!
God saw what he'd made
and said: "Hey, that's not bad!"

In six days God made the world,
and he made it the best,

On the seventh day,
having finished,
he decided to rest.

It's important
to note here,

it's important
to see,

That God, when he made man, said,
"I'll make him like me!"

You were made to make things!
You were formed to create!
God gave you the talent,
don't sit back and wait!

Use the mind you were given
and your crackerjack wit.

Film a big-time production
from your own movie script!

You could make lemonade,
and sell it real cheap,

Or build a small city
where little folks sleep.

ZAP
hardwar
ibrary
school

You could build a big castle
and pretend you're the king,

Then have your friends over
for a midsummer's fling!

You could count your own freckles:
four-hundred-eighty zillion!
Or bake a big pie
with a whole lot of fillin'!

You could name all your toes:
Pops, Pat, Poe, Peg, Pete!
Then you'd have a big party
where once were your feet!

Or pretend you're an astronaut
just drifting through space.

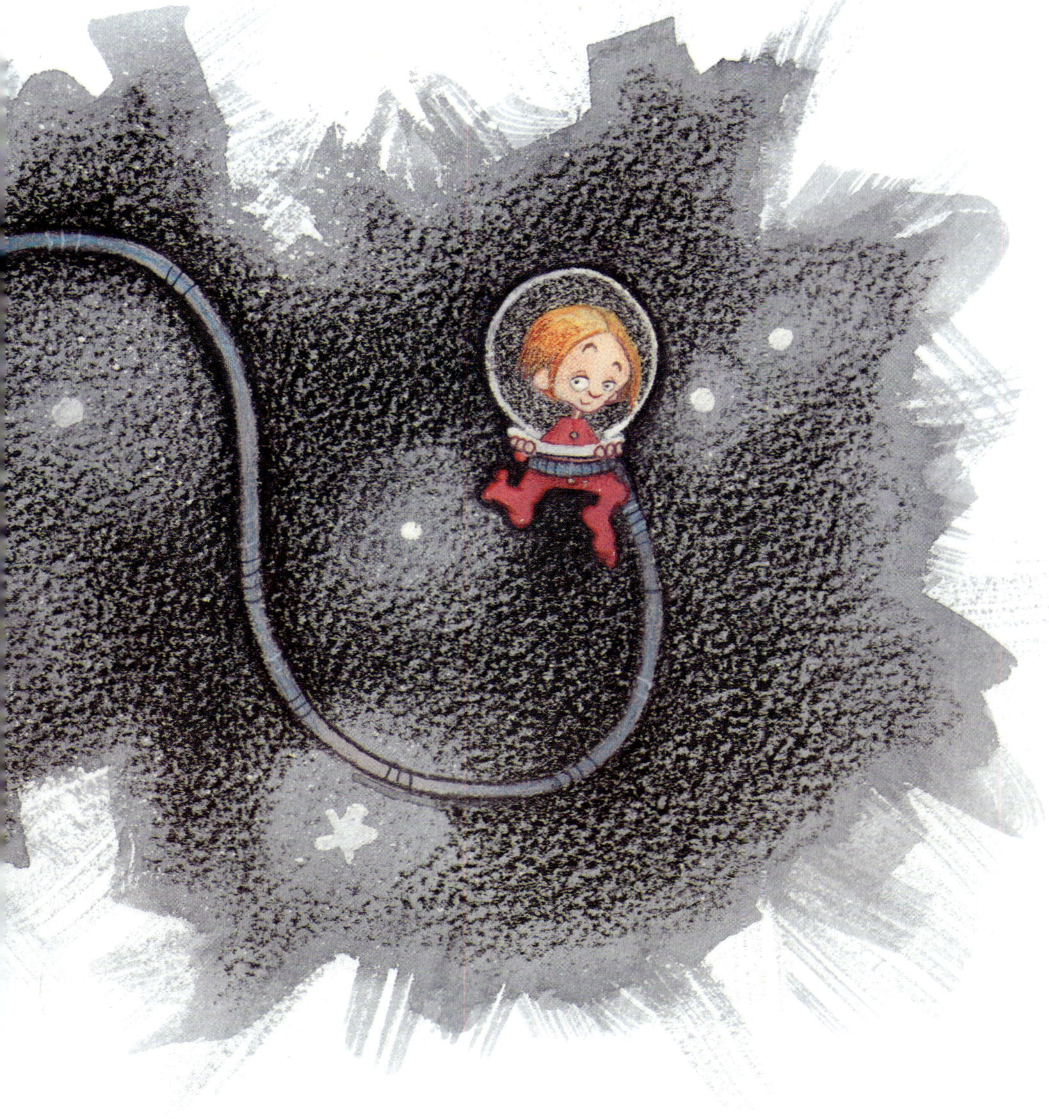

And your sisters are aliens
with a galaxy base.

You could prance like a deer!
You could roar like a lion!

Or pretend you were dad
and put his big tie on!

You could put on an opera
and sing for the masses
in a voice so darn high
you'd break everyone's glasses!

So when you feel blah,
days drag on, and you're bored,
remember this fact, kid:
you were made like the Lord.

And don't you forget,
when there seems
nothing new,

That it was God who
made nothing into
something to do!